100%
SUCCESS
MINDSET

Motivational keys to achieve your goals and

improve your personal development.

© **Samuel C. A.**

For those who gave me strength:

I want to show gratitude to all the people who didn't believe in me. And also to all those who wished to see me fail. Because it was from those feelings that I got the strength to get back on my feet. Do you see me? Yes, I'm still standing!

Samuel

CONTENT

BRIEF INTRODUCTION

Through this book, I merely intend to contribute with my small grain of sand.

It is difficult to innovate in this world, where practically everything has already been said—and has been said in a very good way.

This isn't a book with fixed strategies, where you are told step by step what you are supposed to do to achieve success. It is a motivational book, or at least that has been my intention in writing it. If that is what you are looking for (motivation), I am sure it will be of great help to you. I don't have the magic secret to success, but I will make you reflect on things that have helped me a lot. And if they have helped me, they will help you too. I am going to teach you how to act in certain situations, how to face others, what attitude to have, how to get strength from where there is none, how not to be afraid, how to get out of your comfort zone, how to improve . . .

I want to make it clear from the outset that I do not claim to be a guru. I don't even come close to the great speakers, mentors, and other experts in the field. I wish I did! They are people I greatly admire and from whom you can learn immeasurable. I recommend you read their books, listen to their audiobooks, watch their lectures . . . if you haven't already done so.

They are teachers who will help you achieve success. They have helped me and continue to help me.

As you read, value, and judge my book, I hope you remember that I do not intend to get rich with it, nor do I intend to seek prestige. One thing I have learned is that you have to be generous and share what you know with others. That is my intention. I read everything I can, from the greats to those who have not yet become great (but will be). And they all—I repeat, **they ALL**—have helped me to a greater or lesser extent. Often, the same things are repeated, but giving them a different approach, a personal approach? That makes the message reach your soul. And if it doesn't, going over concepts can never be a negative thing. At least not if those concepts are productive.

But then, who am I?

I am a humble person. I'm not a millionaire, nor do I have the secret of success locked away, wanting to tell everyone about it. But make no mistake, I am no failure. I've had my own successes in life, and I'm still working to have many more and reach the top.

Imagine you are someone who has nothing and has hit rock bottom. Imagine that you have no resources but a multitude of problems (economic, social . . .), a scarcity mindset, you have always gone from failure to failure, and you have never succeeded in anything . . . Raise it to the square, and now make a life for yourself to be successful.

Difficult, isn't it? Well, that's me. Or, rather, it was.

I collected problems. Some came on their own and others I brought on myself. Nobody thought much of me, and what a good thing they did. Life had treated me badly and I treated myself even worse.

Little by little, step by step, I got out of everything, physically and psychologically. Things were moving forward and I tried not to lose motivation. I read books, listened to audio books . . . and put into practice everything I learned. I saw results (slow, but there were results) so that motivated me to continue. I had some ups and downs, I'm not going to fool you, but I kept going and I didn't give up.

> **Slow progress is still progress.**

I emerged from all the bad things. I joined the Army, worked very hard, and was a good soldier. I started playing a lot of sports and even competed in races. I wasn't the best, but I was certainly better. I ran half marathons and 10Ks, as many as I could, every weekend, and I trained every day running 25Ks. For many people, it may not seem like much, but it is for someone who once almost threw up doing a sprint. I continue to run and do a lot of sport, although not as intensely because of a knee injury.

Now I am my own boss. I get up every morning excited about going to work, I don't mind the hours at work and on Sundays, I don't get depressed at the thought of having to work the next day—quite the opposite.

Are you going to tell me that this is not success? For me, it is. But it's not the end. I'm still fighting. I keep moving forward.

> **may not be there yet, but I'm a little closer than I was yesterday.**

I want to add one more thing. And that is that you may now have more reason to think that I have nothing to contribute. But I trust you will be humble and agree with me that everyone learns something from everyone. And I thank you for your attention.

If, like me, you come from nothing, welcome. I hope I can help you find the motivation you need. You'll agree with me that most books are geared towards people who already have some success, but what about those of us who really have nothing? Now that's a challenge! My friend, I'm telling you it can be done!

If there is one thing that all personal development coaches, speakers, writers, and other experts agree on, it is that in order to succeed, you have to fail. And I am an expert in that, so who better than me to write this book?

Are you up for reading it?

Thank you!

WHAT IS SUCCESS?

Before we start spouting the typical motivational stuff about success, let's first stop for a few moments to understand what success is and how it works, or rather, how it acts on us.

This is a part that I personally miss in other books on the same subject.

First of all, what is success? Can you tell me?

Here are some dictionary definitions:

1. Happy result of a business deal, performance, etc.
2. Good acceptance of someone or something.
3. End or completion of a business or matter.

The truth is that it's a bit discouraging, don't you think?

I guess that's not exactly what you're looking for in a motivational book, is it? No worries. Houses aren't meant to start at the roof. This has been the foundation. Now we will move forward.

I imagine that the first thing you have thought of is that for you, success is not something so simple. For you, as for me, it is much more than "the completion of a matter." Am I right?

Success is much more. It is achieving your dream, it is the reward for a hard and prolonged effort, it is happiness, freedom, getting what you want, transcending in life.

What does Wikipedia—an "encyclopedia" full of personal opinions—tell us about it?

Success can mean:

- *Victory (triumph).*
- *A level of social status.*
- *The accomplishment of a goal/objective.*
- *The opposite of failure.*
- *A supermarket chain in Colombia (Éxito).*

These definitions are closer to the concept of what you understand as success, aren't they? At least in my case, it is so (except for the last one, of course).

Below, I will share some answers from a small survey I conducted on my Facebook account, in which I asked some of my followers what success means to them.

- "It boils down to having a peaceful old age with a secure future." (A.Y.)
- "Going to bed and sleeping peacefully." (S. A.)
- "To overcome obstacles and adversities. To be healthy and happy in life." (J. C.)
- "To be happy and have stability." (E. A.)
- "To achieve your goals once they are established." (A. P.)

- "Achieving goals, short or long term, with satisfaction. To feel proud of reaping the fruits harvested and to keep going without stopping. That is a great success. Reaching the top." (Y. V.)
- "To obtain a result through constancy and perseverance." (H. P.)
- "Achievement of goals and realization of projects." (C. S.)
- "Achieving what I want." (J. G.)
- "For me it's having a long and prosperous life. Doing what you like to do and learning to live with all beings, whether they are good or bad. Also, to achieve success would be to know and love yourself and then success would come by itself." (T. E.)

I could share more answers, but I guess it is not necessary. What I intend with this is to show that success does not mean the same for some as it does for others. That is why, in my book, I am not going to focus on a specific model of success, such as financial success, which is the most common in this type of book.

Success is different for different people. You may be looking for financial freedom, or your goal may be something more spiritual. Whatever it is, I am sure it is very important to you.

The mindset, and the guidelines to follow to achieve it, are similar in all cases. At the end of the day, it's about achieving success, getting out of your comfort zone, and having the courage to go for it.

What all respondents do agree on, as you can see, is that success is the result of effort and that, therefore, it is not easy to get there. You have to work hard and not stray from the path.

How does success affect us?

Every time we succeed in something, a biochemical change occurs in our body. At the same time, this causes our dopamine levels to rise.

What is dopamine? Dopamine is a neurotransmitter that is present in various areas of the brain and is especially important for the motor function of the organism. Dopamine activates the neuronal circuits with which we elaborate plans, objectives, strategies, etc.

Being successful (winning, achieving an accomplishment, getting away with something . . .) produces a reaction in our mind that prepares us to be successful again.

Dopamine activates our brain reward circuit, an area that makes us feel pleasure, desire, and motivation. It motivates us to repeat. If we have succeeded once, we will want to succeed more times.

As a result, the next time we succeed, it will be even more rewarding. Not surprisingly, people who are successful from a young age, no matter how insignificant those accomplishments are, will undoubtedly reap more successes throughout their lives. They will seek them out, and they will do whatever it takes to get them.

Success, then, makes us feel great. Did you know that it shares brain circuits with sex? It also eliminates fears, anxiety, and depression. Success improves our cognitive abilities and makes us much more creative.

A JOURNEY OF A THOUSAND MILES BEGINS WITH A SINGLE STEP.

Lao-tsé

We are often overwhelmed when we have to embark on the road to our goal or objective. We see it as far away, practically unreachable. We have to take many steps to get there. That requires effort, sacrifice, constancy, dedication, perseverance, uncertainty . . . and time, above all, time. We want what we long for right now. This uncontrollable desire to reach our goal makes us become impatient, anxious, and irrational.

Don't get me wrong, it is completely understandable that you want to achieve your purpose as soon as possible, enjoy it, and experience that comforting sensation that you feel when you get something after much effort and sacrifice. You want that moment when you are happy, as if it were a lottery prize, but even more rewarding on an emotional level, because you know that you deserve it and that you have worked hard to get it. In fact, it is not productive not to feel that desire, that desire to achieve it, because it is precisely that desire that will give you enough energy to achieve what you set out to achieve.

The goal is not reached with an apathetic and conformist attitude. The only thing you have to do is channel all that energy and focus on your goal and what the steps are to follow to reach it.

A journey of a thousand miles begins with the first step, and then comes another, and another, and then another, and then another. Do you know where you have to go? Do you know where to put your foot on the next step? No? Well, first, figure it out. If you know, go for it! You'll be one step closer to the finish line.

Do you see it far away? It will always be just as far away if you don't start now.

But I understand you. To lose those extra pounds, it will take months; to write your book will take much longer; to successfully finish college, years; to become Arnold Schwarzenegger, much longer!

Phew, you get tired just thinking about it, don't you?

I'm going to tell you a little secret, but don't tell anyone, okay?

Time will pass anyway

That's right. In the midst of so much overwhelm and fear of starting, it had slipped your mind, hadn't it? Don't worry. This, like many other things in the book, is a thought that is there, that we all know, but that we don't take into account. That's what I'm here for, to remind you and show you the way.

And the fact is that time will run no matter what. Time won't care if you start studying or not; it will follow its path, second by second, minute by minute, hour by hour . . .

You can choose to start to achieve your goal or not, but time will pass anyway. How long does the career you want to study at the university take? Four years? "Yes, and four years is a very long time. I can't wait that long," you might say.

Well, think about one thing: the four years will pass anyway, whether you study or not. Do you know what the difference is? In four years, you can have your career or not have it and be exactly the same as you are now.

Do you want to lose weight? How many times have you said, "I would have to . . ." or "I am going to . . ." and in the end, you have done nothing? How many times have you thought that if you had started with what you set out to do, you would have achieved your goal by now? You just had to take the first step.

> **Sometimes, a step in the right direction can end up being the biggest step of your life.**

●●●

A very peculiar hiker, missing his left leg, which he had lost years ago in a car accident, decided to climb to the top of Mount Everest—no less.

He prepared everything he needed for his adventure, he made up his mind, and, rejecting all possible help and accompaniment, he set out to crown that majestic peak.

No one believed he could make it, some could not let go of their worries, but that man made it to the top.

Yes, he made it!

You can imagine, dear reader, the media commotion that ensued. All the television and radio stations and newspapers were scrambling to interview him.

At a press conference, one journalist asked him: "Excuse me for asking, but considering that you are missing a leg, how did you make it to the top?"

To which the main character of such an incredible feat answered:

"Step by step. I arrived step by step."

●●●

And this is how everything is achieved, going step by step. But for that, you always have to take the first one. The rest will come later.

Make the decision, don't look so far ahead, and enjoy the journey. Each thing you do, in relation to your goal, will bring you closer to it. After one step comes another, and then another. Focusing on those steps, giving 100% of yourself in each one of them, will make the road more bearable. They are small goals that you will achieve, small grains of sand that will eventually form a mountain. If you see them as achievements, however small they may be, you will be brimming with motivation.

If you decide to start a university career, don't think of it as a whole; focus on each course as a goal to achieve. After that will come another course and, when you pass it, then another one. Divide that goal, which is the course, into smaller goals, which can be the exams and papers you have to complete. Moreover, each topic of each subject can be a challenge, a goal to achieve. The satisfaction you will experience when you feel that you have achieved your goal, when you learn a subject, will motivate you to continue and will tell your subconscious that you are on the right track, that you are doing well, that you will succeed. Go for the next one!

If you've set out to lose weight, your micro-goals can be every single day you successfully make it through the diet, or every small percentage of body fat you lose. Don't dwell on your final goal, getting overwhelmed because you're not there yet, thinking about how much or how little is left. Enjoy the process and all those little achievements, which will inevitably give you that final result you want so much.

> **Take the first step in faith. You don't need to see the whole staircase, just take your first step.**
>
> Martin Luther King

Now you know what you have to do. Make up your mind and don't fall into the uncomfortable situation of wondering what would have happened if you had taken that path, regretting that you have wasted your time—valuable time that will never come back.

Imagine yourself for a moment in that situation. Yes, I know I should be trying to motivate you, and that thought isn't exactly very motivating, I admit. But trust me, how long do you think it might take you to achieve your goal? A year, four years, maybe more? Well, now imagine yourself in that time—let's say four years—without having taken that first step, having abandoned your dream because you saw it as too far away and unattainable. You don't have it, but you still want it. You think about it constantly. Often, you decide that you could still get on with it, but it's been so long, hasn't it? If you had started when you first thought about it . . .

Time has passed anyway; do you understand now? You just had to take the first step, that's all. Well, and the ones that come after, but we'll talk about that later. The important thing now is that you leave your comfort zone, that you hear the starting gun and go for your dream!

> **Don't cry looking back; better smile taking a step forward.**

STOP THINKING ABOUT LIMITATIONS AND START THINKING ABOUT POSSIBILITIES

Ferry Josephson

"I just can't," "I'll have to stop going to the bar with my friends," "I'll have to do it in my free time . . ."

Sound familiar? I'm sure it does.

Relax, I don't mean to criticize you—it's happened to me too, but there comes a time in life when you have to change your mind. Do you think those are the thoughts of a winner, of a successful being? No! Of course not. That's how a mediocre being thinks, and that's how he goes, living in mediocrity, and you are not a mediocre being, you are a successful being. How do I know? Look at you. What are you doing right now? Looking for success. You are taking your first steps to reach your goals. Do you think that is the attitude of a mediocre being? Of course not!

Now, how should we act if we are successful and triumphant beings? By forgetting the limitations and focusing on the possibilities. Do not think about the things that prevent you from doing it, looking for excuses. Think about all that you will receive by achieving your dream.

Depending on your goal:

- I will be more educated
- I will look thinner
- I will look more muscular
- I will be able to work in what I like
- I will be able to be calm at the end of the month
- I will travel all over
- My children will lack nothing
- I will win some trophies
- I will have the car of my dreams
- I will buy that house I see every day when I come home from work
- I will discover a new vaccine and save many lives
- I will run a marathon
- Many people will read my book
- I will not worry about my bills
- I will live longer and better

You see, just like that, almost without thinking, we can find many more things that benefit us than those that limit us in achieving success. And how pleasant and invigorating it is to think in such a positive way—isn't it?

•••

A long time ago, a little boy named Tim visited the circus for the first time. He enjoyed the show immensely. What struck him most was the appearance of various animals, performing all sorts of exercises and juggling.

There was one animal, in particular, that caught his attention. It was enormous. The boy had never seen an animal of that size before. I'm sure you know what animal I'm talking about, don't you? Exactly! The elephant.

When the show was over, the boy asked his parents if they could go to the area where the animals were kept. He wanted to see the huge animal again.

Suddenly, Tim noticed that the elephant was chained to a small stake driven into the ground. It was obvious that this security measure was designed to prevent the animal from escaping.

Nevertheless, Tim kept thinking about it. Something was wrong. The chain holding the animal's leg had a rigid appearance and was undoubtedly of a thickness that was safe enough for that use. However, that tiny stake ... How could that small piece of wood hold an animal of that size? The truth is that the elephant did not even make any attempt to break free. Considering its size and strength, it should be able to uproot a tree, and had it never tried to break free from that ridiculous restraint?

Intrigued, he asked his father, who claimed not to have noticed this, and went on to say, "Tim, can't you see that the elephant is trained?" "Ah," Tim replied.

But the little boy's conviction didn't last long. He immediately added, "Then, Daddy, why are they chaining him up?"

Before Tim's bewildered father could utter a word, an elderly man, who had been listening in on the whole conversation, said to the boy:"So he doesn't forget his limitations and doesn't begin to think about the possibilities. He has been tied to that stake since he was a little cub. Back then, he tried to escape, day after day, night after night. Those limitations became fixed in his mind, and he stopped trying. Now he could escape, but he thinks he can't."

●●●

Don't be like the elephant. The limitations that once prevented you from achieving your dream may not be so now. Try again. Think of the possibilities. Perhaps you were not motivated at the time, you did not find the key, or you did not know how to find a solution. I am not saying that you did not have real limitations—everyone lives their own life and knows what they have been through and the circumstances in which they have found themselves. But many times, there are paths that can take us out of that point, we just don't see them. Often, we have to re-examine our objectives to see them from a new perspective, with a different mentality, in another moment of our life. Maybe there are no such limitations now. Remember the elephant. He could let go of his bonds, but he had stopped trying; he thought he could not, and he did not think of the possibilities, only of the limitations.

> **Decide to see each problem as a possibility to find a solution.**

Every problem is a challenge. It's just something that stands between you and success. Don't get angry, don't get upset. That only makes us less clear-headed, and it will take longer to find the solution. There's a problem? Perfect! Let's get rid of it. Let's solve it. Remember that you are an achiever, a successful being, you are not just anybody. Successful people like a challenge—they don't take the easy way out.

There is only one thing in this life that has no solution, and I think you already know what it is, so there is no need to mention it. Everything else has a solution; you get out of everything, faster or slower, but you get out. You just have to get down to work and get a good grip on yourself. That little thing is the only thing that can make you succeed, nothing else. And, note, I said "slow down," not avoid. Once you have solved your little mishap, you will have a clear path to your dream.

Isn't it motivating? You will also feel fulfilled and you will be more convinced that you can do anything, and no one and nothing can stop you. You are on your way to success!

> **Limits, like fears, are often just an illusion.**
> Michael Jordan

THE ONLY IMPOSSIBLE THING IS THAT WHICH YOU DO NOT TRY

One of the most serious defects of human beings is to give up before we have even started. We give up before we have even tried.

How can we be so weak? And I include myself, because it wouldn't be honest to say that it has never been me. But I got tired a long time ago of having that attitude. I got tired of predicting non-existent failures and, therefore, of feeling like a failure. I realized that I was trying to run away from that failure when what I was really doing was failing for not having tried.

That is the real defeat. We limit ourselves and clip our own wings. We are solely responsible for not being where we want to be. Then we blame "this" and "that" or, much worse, "that" or "the other."

Don't give up without trying. As they say, the "no" is already there. Not reaching your goal is the easiest thing in the world. In fact, in that, you are guaranteed success if you want it. Just don't do anything, and I give you my word that the only thing you will have succeeded at is not having succeeded.

Action is necessary to achieve success. You have to set in motion the whole process necessary to reach your destination. Sometimes, we see something as totally impossible when, in fact, if we do what it takes, it is the opposite of that—i.e., totally impossible that it is impossible. In fact, there's no way it won't happen.

You don't believe me? I imagine you are thinking that it is mere talk, typical of self-help and self-improvement books. Well, I assure you that's what I'm telling you. If you take all the steps to get somewhere, or make all the decisions focused on achieving something, you will inevitably get there. And I want to repeat once again that it is totally inevitable, to make it very clear. Even if you decide that you don't want it, if you have followed the specific guidelines for it, it will come, it will happen, you will get it.

If you are looking for success, you will get it anyway, even if you regret it at the last minute and decide not to have it. Let me convince you of that with a few examples:

- Imagine that for an entire summer, you go to the beach every day. You go every day from sunrise to sunset. You don't use an umbrella (but remember to wear sunscreen). Inevitably, your skin is going to tan, whether you want it to or not.

- You set out on a low-calorie diet. You go jogging for an hour every day. You supplement with fat burners and natural diuretics, such as caffeine, green tea, cayenne, ginger, and dandelion. You will inevitably lose weight. Even if you want to get fat, that won't happen, because you have done everything necessary to lose weight and will inevitably do it.

- You read a book every week and in your free time, you watch a documentary video. You do this for five years in a row. Inevitably, you will learn many things. You cannot follow these habits and decide not to learn, because it is impossible for you not to learn.

Do you understand now that the impossible is not reaching your goal? It is a matter of time. Depending on what you want to achieve, among other factors, it will take more or less time to arrive, but it will inevitably arrive. Stop thinking that it is impossible. You just need to follow the right steps and not give up. And, by all means, don't give up before you've even started.

●●●

It was a day of celebration in the frog village. As usual, all kinds of festivities, performances, meals, and even sporting events were organized on the occasion of the celebrations.

Every year, new activities were proposed. That year, it was agreed that, in the field of sports, a foot race would be held. The start would take place at the village pond, and the finish line would be at the top of the mountain. That mountain presented great difficulties in its ascent, with a steep terrain and a slope that gave vertigo just looking at it. To all this, we had to add the long distance. At first, some frogs were opposed to the idea and tried to agree on a simpler route, but one of the frogs, very proud, said: "What is happening is that you are afraid. You know that no one in the village is capable of beating me. We will hold the race on the agreed course. I am so sure of winning that if any frog beats me, I will work for them as a servant for a year."

The rest of the frogs, who could not stand the attitude of their companion, accepted the proposal only in the hopes of seeing him lose.

The day of the race arrived and there was much anticipation to watch the event. A crowd of frogs crowded at the start, and a large number of frogs lined the course.

The race started, and all the frogs hurried to the top of the mountain. The frogs in the audience cheered on the competitors.

The kilometers passed, and little by little, some frogs were slowly dropping out. It was a very hard race. But others continued with enthusiasm.

The terrain became more and more impracticable, and the slope became steeper and steeper. Few frogs were still holding on. Gradually, the voices of the audience changed to a less hopeful kind of message."It's too hard! You won't make it!" shouted the frogs watching the race.

Before long, only five frogs were enduring the exhausting effort. One of them was the braggart who had claimed he would win the race.

Thus, three of them fell down from exhaustion along the way. Some of them had to be treated by the emergency medical services. But the show-off frog and another one did not give up.The audience cried out, "Can't you see you can't get to the top? Give up now! It's impossible to get up there!"

The cocky frog didn't want to give up, even though he couldn't go any further. But as he watched his rival climb up and up to the top of the mountain, without looking back, he thought it would be a humiliation to give up now.

The observers insisted:"For God's sake! It's totally impossible! It can't be done! It's better to give up now and avoid a scare! No one can do it!"

The boastful frog, much to his dismay, collapsed to the ground, exhausted beyond belief. But his opponent kept climbing up the mountain. She climbed and climbed until she reached the top. She seemed to ignore the words of the others.

At the end of the race, the winner was awarded a trophy, and everyone wanted to greet her and congratulate her. The frog was then found to be deaf and had not heard anyone during the race.

●●●

How did she do it? She didn't know it was impossible.

> **Since I didn't know it was impossible, I did it.**
> Albert Einstein

IF YOU ALWAYS TRY TO BE NORMAL, YOU WILL NEVER DISCOVER HOW EXTRAORDINARY YOU CAN BE

Maya Angelou

There is one thing you have to be clear about and never forget, and that is that if you do normal things, you will be a normal person. Does someone normal seem like an achiever to you? Someone ordinary? Just another one? Certainly not. Successful people are successful because, at a certain point in their lives, they decided to break away from the normal, from the established.

Think about your day-to-day life, everything you do: you get up, have breakfast, go to work, come home, have dinner, read a book or watch your favorite TV show, go to bed . . . Is it something like that?

Now think about your goal, what you want to achieve, that moment of success. Why aren't you there yet? Because you are following a normal routine. Change—change it all. Get up half an hour earlier, forget about the TV, and get to work on your goal.

While others are on the couch or in bed, you should be writing your book or documenting yourself for it; you can be studying to reach that academic level you want; you will have time to go for a run or do some exercises, if what you want is a better physique, or to improve your sports practice; you can be looking for information to help you achieve your goals (books, videos, conferences, seminars, podcasts, blogs, websites, etc.).

Think for a moment about the sentence that heads this chapter: "... you will never discover how extraordinary you can be."

What does the concept of "extraordinary" mean?

Let's see what the dictionary says about it:

"Outside the natural or common order or rule."

Out of the established—in short, out of the ordinary.

What do you now think you have to do to become extraordinary? Exactly! Not act normal, not be normal, and not do what is supposed to be normal.

> **To be irreplaceable, one must always seek to be different.**
>
> Coco Chanel

Do you think Coco Chanel would have been successful if she had been satisfied with being normal? She managed to break into the business world, and considering that she was a woman in the early twentieth century, that is worthy of admiration—I say this in reference to the social rejection of women at that time, especially in the field of business. How did she do it? By going out of the ordinary.

She invented women's sportswear, her famous suit jacket, imitated to this day; she kept her hair short, making this style fashionable; she created the revolutionary women's pants; she made tanning fashionable; she invented costume jewelry, making jewelry available to all women, and created her best-known product, the perfume Chanel n°5, which was the first to incorporate synthetic substances.

All very normal for the time, right?

The famous French novelist, Victor Hugo, author of such classics as Les Miserables, made an unusual decision to meet the deadline for the delivery of his work, Notre Dame de Paris. He got rid of all his clothes and firmly ordered his servants to hide them and not to give him anything until he had finished his work. He then locked himself in his room.

Victor Hugo managed to deliver his work several weeks before the deadline.

Do you have clothes to get rid of? You can use it as a metaphor. Adapt the idea to your situation and goal. Hide your clothes and don't take them out until you have achieved your purpose. It can be your favorite TV series or program, your evenings with friends, the weekend soccer games, some treat . . .

Think for a moment of Salvador Dalí, the Spanish painter with a totally surrealist style. Not only his creations were out of the ordinary. He flaunted his flamboyant personality. He was a complete package. He was selling his brand. Do you think he would have gotten so far drawing a simple still life?

And with a more normal personality? Surely, for his artistic technique, he would have stood out, but, without a doubt, his flamboyant and outlandish personality catapulted him to fame.

What about the first person who wanted to fly? And the first person who wanted to reach the moon? And the first person who wanted to cross the Atlantic Ocean? Do you think they were taken for normal people?

You were born to be extraordinary! To be extraordinary, you just need to do extraordinary things, out of the ordinary. To think differently from others, to do what others do not do and, in short, to be different from others, different from the majority of people.

Most people don't read self-improvement books, nor do they look for inspiration or motivation to improve themselves. In fact, many people don't even read at all.

Most people do not spend time thinking about solutions and tools to achieve their goals. A lot of people don't even get to the point of setting goals.

Most people don't try to get out of their comfort zone; they are content with what they have, and yet they envy their neighbor for all that they have achieved. And they wish they had the same, but they do absolutely nothing to achieve it.

Most people do NOTHING to improve themselves.

Do you realize now how extraordinary you are? You have dreams. You are looking for ways to achieve them. You are determined and 100% committed to achieve success. And you are not lying on the couch, complaining about your bad luck and criticizing your neighbor's good luck. You, for that alone, are already extra-ordinary.

> ## The difference between ordinary and extraordinary is that little bit extra.
> Jimmy Johnson

You can succeed by preparing for it in an extraordinary way, working for it in an extraordinary way, investing for it in an extraordinary way, planning for it in an extraordinary way . . . and going for it in an extraordinary way!

Your destiny is to be extraordinary.

My advice is to tell yourself everyday, "I am extraordinary." And it's not enough to say it—you have to feel it.

· In the morning, when you wake up, say: "I am extraordinary!" And feel it, think about why you are extraordinary. You will start the day by programming your mind with that belief.

· Throughout the day, say: "I am extraordinary!" Say it in the car on the way to work; say it in the shower; say it when you walk down the street . . . Yes, I know you don't intend to be taken for a fool. If there are people in front of you, or you can't say it out loud, say it mentally, but as if you were saying it out loud, shouting it.

· Take every possible opportunity to tell yourself that you are extraordinary. And believe that it is so. Say it over and over again, if necessary changing or adding words, even emphasizing the message. I am fucking extraordinary!

· Before going to sleep, say: "I am extraordinary!" Say it already in bed, before going to sleep, and think of everything you have done during the day to be so extraordinary. Whatever you have been able to do, if you have done it in an extraordinary way, you are already extraordinary. You are not a normal person; you are not ordinary. You are no longer like most people. Meditate on this and you will fall asleep with the mindset of an achiever. It is inevitable that these thoughts will remain engraved in your subconscious, and your mental reprogramming oriented to achieve success will be set in motion.

Do you think I have written the word "extraordinary" too many times throughout the chapter? That's precisely what it's about, that this word—or, better said, what it means—is engraved in your subconscious.

> **One machine can do the work of fifty ordinary men, but no machine can do the work of one extraordinary man.**
> Elbert Hubbard.

Don't settle for normal. Focus on being so much more than you are now. Focus on being extraordinary.

90% OF SUCCESS IS BASED SIMPLY ON INSISTING

Woody Allen

You get success by working hard. It is not like roulette in a casino, where you try to see if you do well, and if not, you throw your hands on your head and go to try your luck at another table or another game.

To achieve success, you have to insist, and a lot. It is not something that comes overnight.

If you ask any successful person or personal development coach, they will all tell you the same thing—that 100% of the people who fail to achieve success do it for the same reason: because they gave up.

Everyone who has made it to the top has done so for one reason: because they never gave up. The road to success is fraught with obstacles and disappointments. Whether you can achieve your goal in life depends on your attitude in the face of those setbacks.

All this will seem obvious to you, but be honest, how many times have you abandoned a project? And now tell me, how many of those projects are you now convinced that you would have completed had you not given up? I raise my hand because I am the first one in that situation. It's all right, we are human beings. But we must be aware of it so that it does not happen again.

We often get overwhelmed, and we see the end of the road far away. And surely it is, but if we give up, not only will it be far away, but we will never get there, and we will also have to live with the thorn in our side of not knowing what would have happened if we had continued, if we had persisted.

When we start with a new goal, we want quick and effortless results, but think about it: is there anything good in life that doesn't cost effort and sacrifice? Everything worthwhile in this world requires dedication and patience. Everything worthwhile will require work on your part to get it. It will not be easy. It means that there will be stumbles, mistakes, frustration, and the desire to give up. It is up to you to rise above it all.

A winner is a loser who never gave up.

There was a time—and this is a true story I'm going to tell you—a man lost his job. He set up his own business, failed, and was ruined. Shortly thereafter, the love of his life died. He suffered a nervous breakdown. He ran for Speaker of the Illinois House of Representatives and lost. Five years later, he lost the nomination for Congress. Five years later, he lost the renomination. Six years passed and he ran for U.S. Senate and lost. Two years later, he lost in the election for vice-presidential candidate. Two more years and he lost the election for the U.S. Senate again.

That stubborn man was Abraham Lincoln, elected president of the United States two years later, in 1860.

As you can see, if Abraham Lincoln had thrown in the towel, he would never have made it as far as he did. And not only was he president of that country, but he remained for posterity as one of the most important U.S. presidents of all time.

Do you really want it? Then you will go for it, and you will not give up. If you're convinced you can do it, you'll keep trying again and again.

Thomas Alva Edison, the well-known inventor with more than 1900 patents on file, spent more than two years trying to find the right filament to make the light bulb work. He was at it, almost without rest, day and night, for about 800 days. He did not give up, because he knew that success would come and that it was only a matter of time. It was just a matter of insisting.

Does this sound like a sign of perseverance? Well, it doesn't stop there. During the whole process, he tried more than 1,000 different filaments. Would you have done the same or would you have given up? What would have happened if he had done it? Surely the light bulb would have been invented, but he wouldn't have done it. Someone else would have taken the credit.

A young journalist approached him for an interview, when he had not yet found the right filament, and asked him:

"Mr. Edison. You've had about 1,000 unsuccessful attempts. Aren't you tired of failing?"

To which Edison replied:

"I haven't failed! I already know about 1,000 ways not to light the light bulb. Therefore, I am about 1,000 times closer to succeeding."

The truly persevering person doesn't accept ultimate failure and gives no importance to the time it will take to achieve success in what he or she desires. The persevering person keeps at it. The time it takes to achieve it is not important. The important thing is to achieve it.

The human being is not defeated until he accepts defeat in his or her own mind.

Another well-known story (and this is the last, I promise) is that of Colonel Sanders, the founder of the Kentucky Fried Chicken (KFC) fast food restaurant chain, who was neither a colonel nor anything like that.

He wanted to sell his fried chicken recipe in a multitude of restaurants, and he was rejected in all of them. But before that, he had also failed miserably in several other businesses.

In this aspect, I could be giving examples until I write a specific book for it. But I think you get the idea from the ones already mentioned, don't you?

There is a very important factor that makes people succeed by insisting, and that is that they create a commitment to their project. They commit themselves to carry it out no matter what happens.

And what is commitment? Well, there is a person I admire very much who usually defines it very well. He is Francisco Alcaide. He is a lecturer, writer, and trainer on leadership and motivation. He has written several books, among which I would like to highlight *Aprendiendo de los mejores* (Alienta Editorial). He describes commitment in the following masterful way:"Commitment is doing whatever it takes, for as long as it takes."

I don't think it can be said more clearly or described more accurately. If you want to succeed, you have to be clear that you are going to have to do whatever it takes and for as long as it takes, otherwise you will fail.

Robert Lee Frost, American poet, said: "In two words I can sum up how much I've learned about life: Keep going."

And it's more of the same. In the end, it's all about persistence, not giving up, not throwing in the towel, not quitting. These are all synonyms for failure, as far as the road to success is concerned. Only the most persistent and the bravest will reach the end of the journey. As Napoleon Bonaparte said, "Courage is not having the strength to go on, it is going on when you no longer have the strength." And also, "My greatness does not lie in never having fallen, but in always having risen."

Never give up and go for your dream. You are capable of anything. Giving up is a thing of lazy people and failures and you are above all that. The mediocre being will constantly look for excuses; the excellent being will find solutions. Everything comes if we are strong enough to move forward.

The saying "he who keeps going gets it" is not just a popular proverb, it is much more. And if, after all this, you don't see it clearly, just trust me. The world is full of successful people who didn't give up and of failures who throw in the towel.

Which side do you want to be on: the road to success or the consequences of failure?

> **Pain is a temporary thing. It may last a minute, an hour, a day, or a year, but eventually it will be gone and something else will take its place. However, if I surrender, that pain will be forever.**
>
> Lance Armstrong

When you think about giving up, remember the reason you started. What got you started? Remember it and keep it in mind. Turn to that thought when you feel weakness. It will give you new energy to continue.

When we are blinded by reaching the end of the road, and it becomes endless because of the stumbling blocks, we often forget the reason why we started, the spark that made us start our adventure. A reason so great that it filled us with dreams and hope and that made us think that everything was possible, that we were going to make it happen.

We remove that idea from our field of vision, and that is one of the mistakes we must avoid making.

I'm sure you've seen, especially in cartoons, the typical horse race, in which the horse has a bracket placed on its head with a carrot hanging in front of its eyes, in the center of its field of vision. The horse runs like hell towards the finish line, without taking his eyes off the carrot. He doesn't care about the other horses, the screams of the people, or that the world is falling down. He only thinks about the carrot. It is the stimulus that got him started, the one that keeps him going without stopping, and the one that will get him to the finish line.

What is your carrot?

YOU TRIED. YOU FAILED. IT DOESN'T MATTER. TRY AGAIN. FAIL AGAIN. FAIL BETTER.

Samuel Beckett

A nyone who wants to avoid failure will inevitably be avoiding success. In order to succeed, it is necessary to fail—and certainly to fail many times.

As Og Mandino, the American writer and author of the bestseller *The World's Greatest Salesman*, once said: "He who never failed is he who never tried."

If you are determined to pay the price for success, you must be determined to accept failure, not as failure, but as a tool or part of the process. As they say, "You learn from your mistakes."

That you are going to have obstacles is practically guaranteed. It is up to you to see them as inconveniences which will slow you down or even stop you on your path to success, or to see them as challenges and opportunities to come out of them stronger.

> **There are no mistakes in life, only learning opportunities.**
>
> Robert Kiyosaki

Making a mistake is the best thing that can happen to you, so you should be glad when it does. On the one hand, and taking into account that we have made it clear that you are going to make a mistake, when you do, it will mean that you have already advanced further towards success. You have already made that mistake—learn from it and keep moving forward. You must analyze each mistake, reflecting on where and why you have made a mistake, and make it serve as a learning experience. Surely you will not make that mistake again, neither in your current project nor in those that may come later.

Henry Ford said: "The only real mistake is the one from which we learn nothing."

As I like to "pull" the dictionary, let's see what the dictionary says about failure: "Adverse result in a business or in achieving or doing something."

And now I repeat, "adverse result." So, what conclusion do we take from all this? Well, we know how not to do it, or what not to do. We have already learned something! That is already an achievement. A success within a failure. Now you must analyze it and find out why that is not the way, and then you will deduce what is the right way, or possible right way—because remember that you may fail again.

Do you understand that it is not the end of the world, but just another stage in the process?

> **Sometimes, by losing a battle,**
> **you find a new way to win the war.**
>
> Donald Trump

Another thing to keep in mind is that, when you fail, you have to become aware of it and admit that you are the only one responsible. You cannot focus on blaming anyone or anything, because then you will not see the need to look for a solution, nor will you learn from it, since, according to you, you were not to blame. If you think it is due to an external factor, you will not correct your mistake.

Get that idea out of your head! As Francisco Alcaide, author of *Aprendiendo de los mejores*, says:"He who falls into the water and drowns doesn't drown because he has fallen into the water, but because he doesn't know how to swim."

●●●

During a scene in the movie *Rocky VI*, Rocky (Silvester Stallone) tells his son:

"You ain't gonna believe this, but you used to fit right here. (He gestures to the palm of his hand). I'd hold you up to say to your mother, 'This kid's gonna be the best kid in the world. This kid's gonna be somebody better than anybody I ever knew.' And you grew up good and wonderful. It was great just watchin' you, every day was like a privilege. Then the time come for you to be your own man and take on the world, and you did. But somewhere along the line, you changed. You stopped being you. You let people stick a finger in your face and tell you you're no good. And when things got hard, you started lookin' for something to blame, like a big shadow.

Let me tell you something you already know.The world ain't all sunshine and rainbows. It's a very mean and nasty place, and I don't care how tough you are, it will beat you to your knees and keep you there permanently if you let it. You, me, or nobody is gonna hit as hard as life. But it ain't about how hard you hit, it's about how hard you can get hit and keep moving forward. How much you can take and keep moving forward. That's how winning is done!

Now if you know what you're worth, then go out and get what you're worth! But you gotta be willing to take the hits. And not pointing fingers saying you ain't where you wanna be because of him, or her, or anybody! Cowards do that and that ain't you! You're better than that!"

– Rocky Balboa

●●●

How do you feel in your body? Inspirational, isn't it? Yes, it is.

Besides, I assure you that blaming your failures will fill you with frustration and helplessness, therefore, with negativity. You will think that you could not have done anything to avoid it, and that you are very "unlucky."

I am going to tell you a story about luck, although it is not the main theme of this chapter of the book. It is a traditional Chinese tale, and it goes like this:

Once upon a time, there was a man whose two great passions in life were his son and his horse.

One day, his horse ran away, and the man was very sad (is it good luck or bad luck?).

After a few days, the horse returned, but not alone. He brought with him a beautiful mare. The man was very happy (is it bad luck or good luck?).

Shortly thereafter, his son went out riding with the mare. In a stumble, he fell off the mare and broke several bones in his body. He was left in bed, in great pain (is it good luck or bad luck?).

While the young man was recovering, a war broke out, and the government was recruiting soldiers in every home. When they arrived at his home, they could not take the young man to the war, as he was badly wounded (is it bad luck or good luck?).

●●●

It all depends. It's neither one thing nor the other. Stop complaining about the circumstances and look on the bright side.

I don't want to go any deeper into this subject because it deviates from the concepts we are dealing with. But I thought it would be interesting to mention this story, and I am sure it will be of great use to you.

We were talking about failure, weren't we? Well, there is little more to say about it. The important thing is that the main points are clear to you:

1. You are going to fail.
2. Learn from it.
3. Don't see failures as defeats or obstacles. Take them as challenges and as a chance to improve.
4. You know how not to do it. Now you are more likely to succeed.

> **Failure is the key to success; every mistake teaches us something.**
>
> Morihei Ueshiba

DO YOU REALLY WANT IT? SO, ARE YOU WILLING TO PAY THE PRICE?

To achieve success in something (whatever it is), what you really have to be very clear about is if you really want it. To do this, you should answer some questions like these:

· Is it your dream?

· Is it what you really want in this life?

· Are you willing to do EVERYTHING it takes to get it?

· Whatever it takes?

· Are you prepared to accept failure and overcome all kinds of adversity?

· Is there any chance, however remote, that you will give up during the process?

· Will you focus 100% on it?

· Will you be able to say NO to whims, likes, hobbies, evenings with friends . . . ?

Be very clear that if you want it, from now on, you will forget everything that has nothing to do with your goal. Time you waste on other things is time you are not advancing. That would mean that it would take you longer to get there and that you would probably be more motivated to give up.

What is your goal? To achieve financial freedom? Or maybe something very different, like winning a sports trophy? Do you think Warren Buffet would play PlayStation in his spare time? Or do you think Usain Bolt would lie on the couch on Sundays and drink a few beers with his buddies?

Success requires sacrifice, and you have to be willing and proud to pay for it to get to the top.

Arnold Schwarzenegger said: "It's important to have fun in life. But while you're out there having a good time, just remember that there's someone somewhere else who's working hard and preparing, someone who's winning. Success is work, a lot of work."

Keep in mind that if you don't fight for your dream, no one else will. And somewhere else, there is another person with the same dream as you, working hard to achieve it. If your goal has a number of reserved places (workplace, sporting merit, best in whatever), think that there is always another person working hard to be there and snatch it away from you. Do not rest on your laurels and sweat blood in it.

It is a pride and joy to pay the price for success. It means that you are closer to achieving it and that it is certain that you are going to achieve it.

Let's imagine that you want to buy a 60" TV, latest model, which has a price of €3.000. Surely it will hurt your wallet when you have to pay that amount (it would hurt me, but there will be those who are thinking that for them it is small change). But what you are sure of is that, once you have the money, the TV will be yours and you will be able to go straight to enjoying it, right?

The same thing happens with success. You have to pay a price. That price is hard work, sacrifice, commitment, effort, perseverance, failure, learning . . . But when you have paid it, you will get in return what you are looking for. It's as simple as that.

Be happy that you are paying the price for success.

Brian Tracy, best-selling author of several personal development books, used to say:"If you want to get in touch with a future billionaire, phone him at his office after hours. You're sure to find him there."

He added:"There are no shortcuts to success. Start earlier, work harder, and finish later."

What all this means is that you not only have to work hard, but you have to work harder than everyone else.

What is success to you? Getting rich? Why do you think not everyone is rich? Do you think you're the only non-rich person who wants to make big money? Why isn't everyone driving a Rolls-Royce and sailing a yacht?

Because it is not easy! Because you have to pay a very high price to achieve it! It causes a lot of laziness. It is easier to regret and envy those who have achieved it.

We like to criticize and conform, assuring ourselves that these people are lucky and that they have been given everything they've ever had. You know what? So what? That reason is the one that takes away your desire to achieve what you want? Let me tell you, that's a stupid thing to say.

On the other hand, although it is true that there are people who have received money from heaven, I assure you that there are many more (almost infinite) who have not. And they have had to earn it. If they can, so can you. I promise you that 99.9% of people can get what they want if they are willing to pay the price (we won't say 100% because it would be unfair, there will always be special cases, although even so, I'm sure they could improve their situation). Life is full of cases in which people have emerged from nothing and have reached where they wanted. Just do a little research on the internet, and you'll see that there are always special cases.

Everything else is just an excuse. Some may have a harder time than others, but everyone gets there sooner or later, if they sacrifice for it.

Anyway, to those who have been showered with money from heaven, do you hold any kind of grudge? What would you do if you won the lottery? Would you say something like, "I don't want the money, I want to earn it honestly"? I don't think so. What if it turns out that they have everything they need because their parents are rich? Does it bother you? It bothered me for a long time. I was wrong. I didn't have the right mentality, even though I thought I did. Wouldn't you like to become one of those rich parents so that your children would never lack for anything? I certainly do. I know how hard it is to make ends meet and not even have enough for diapers and to think about whether you will be able to give your child the best in life: the best education, the best health care . . .

I apologize for having focused on the financial issue. I know that some readers will have other types of goals, as I have tried to make clear throughout the book. But it is a very clear example of success and, even if your goal is not financial, I highly doubt that you have not agreed with me on everything I have said.

We should not think only of ourselves. By being successful, we also make those around us happy.

**If you don't fight today,
don't cry tomorrow.**

GET OUT OF YOUR COMFORT ZONE. YOU CAN ONLY GROW IF YOU ARE WILLING TO BE UNCOMFORTABLE AND ANNOYED WHEN TRYING SOMETHING NEW.

Brian Tracy

Everything explained above can be summarized in a very simple way:

Leave your comfort zone.

That is:

- Start
- Break with limitations
- Try
- Stop always doing the same thing
- Insist
- Overcome failures
- Pay the price
- And more

The first thing you have to do is get out of your comfort zone or safety zone.

Before I continue, once again I will resort to the dictionary
to be clear about the concept of **comfort**:
"Welfare or material comfort."

Well-being, comfort . . . In your comfort zone is where you feel good, comfortable, calm, safe, etc.

Let me tell you that you're doing very well there, because nothing is going to happen—don't worry. You won't have to take risks, you won't have to be uncomfortable, you won't have to struggle, you won't have to fail, and you won't have to succeed.

Of course, we have already made it clear that to be successful in life, you need to go through all of the above and much more.

Failure, effort, commitment, hard work, perseverance, implementation of new habits . . . All this is uncomfortable, so people decide that it is better not to succeed. They regret not having it, but it is much more comfortable to go on without it. Or so it is assumed, because, honestly, I find it much more uncomfortable to spend my whole life regretting it and to grow old thinking about what would have happened if I had been brave enough and had not been so lazy and cowardly. And sorry for those words, but that's how it is.

Lack of enthusiasm and fear are the two main reasons that prevent us from leaving our comfort zone.

Idleness:

It happens when you are too lazy to go through all the trouble. Why so much effort if you are already well? Achieving success will take time and dedication, and you'd rather enjoy life, right?

That is something totally respectable. There are those who decide to do nothing and just let time pass. They like to enjoy every moment without obligations. I think that's fine, if that's what you want, but then don't come saying that you haven't achieved anything, or that you want "this" or "that." Enjoying life does not lead to success, nor to anything else, really.

Besides, I personally prefer to enjoy life once I have achieved success. It looks so much better, don't you think?

> **You can't climb the ladder of success with your hands in your pockets.**
> Arnold Schwarzenegger

What's your excuse? Are you bedridden and unable to move? If not, I don't know what you're waiting for to get going. All you have to do is walk the road, that's all. Is it expensive? Of course! But you'll have to do it if you really want to change your life.

Idleness is one of the worst evils of this world. Imagine a humanity without laziness. We would already be light years ahead in evolution from where we are now. Imagine if every person had the will and desire to reach the maximum—the maximum in medicine, in art, in technology, people trying to make this world a better place . . .

Well, you know what? There are already people like that, people willing to give their all for something and reach the top—in short, willing to achieve success whatever the price.

Do you want to succeed? Yes? Are you 100% sure? If so, it won't cost you anything to do whatever it takes. You will do it with enthusiasm and energy, without complaining about how hard it may be.

If you feel too lazy to embark on the road to success, with all its consequences, let me tell you something:

You don't really want it.

I'm sorry to be so harsh, but that's the way it is. I'm not going to argue that you don't want to be successful, whether it's having more money, being a champion in your sport, or making the best potato omelet in the world. But what is clear to me is that you don't want it enough, because if you did, you wouldn't see a problem with it.

If you're not like that, forget everything I've told you, because it wasn't meant for you. If you go for it, with what it takes, you've got the attitude it takes to succeed, and I'm sure you can make it.

Do you agree? Repeat out loud (as if you're angry), loudly, forcefully, energetically:

I'm going to make it! I'm going to succeed!

There is a very simple way to know if you really want to make it to the top:

· <u>If it is your dream:</u> you will find motivation, solutions to the problems, you will start with enthusiasm and grand hopes . . . · <u>If it is just a whim, if it is not your true desire:</u> you will only find excuses.

Fear:

The other main reason why we don't make our dreams come true and which prevents us from stepping out of our comfort zone is fucking fear.

We are terrified of countless things when it comes to undertaking a serious project, such as these:

- Will I fail?
- Will I end up worse off than I am now?
- What will they say about me if I do?
- What will they say about me if I don't succeed?
- Will I lose my money/time/dignity . . . ?
- Will I be able to?
- Won't it be too risky?
- What will happen if I don't succeed?

Maybe you are one of those who ask themselves these kinds of questions and decide to live your whole life without finding the answers and you know what? There is a way to know them. You know how? Dare to do it!

Besides, if you don't make that decision and get out of your comfort zone, you will always be asking yourself the worst question of all:

What would have happened if I had been brave enough to try it?

There is a very popular phrase that an old man taught me, which fits this whole story: "The only thing I regret in this life is what I have NOT done."

> **When you see a successful business, someone once made a difficult decision about the business.**
>
> Peter Drucker

On the road to success, it happens as in poker or in investments: to win, it is necessary to take risks. But that does not necessarily mean failure.

When you take a risk, there are chances of success and chances of failure, but people tend to think directly of risk as an imminent failure, which is a very negative way of thinking because we forget that there are also chances of success. Why don't we focus on that option instead of failure? In fact, if we do things moderately well, it is unlikely that something catastrophic will happen, don't you think?

> **If you're not willing to risk the unusual, you'll have to settle for the ordinary.**
>
> Jim Rohn

Having said all this, if you do not decide to leave your comfort zone, it will be due to at least one of the following causes:

You are lazy (**idleness**). You are a coward (**fear**).

Tough and direct, right? If you've read other personal development or motivational books, you're not used to it, but that's precisely what's wrong with those books. They're not entirely honest with you. Don't get me wrong, as I said at the beginning, those books are infinitely better than this one you have in your hands, there is no doubt about that. But personally, I haven't found any of them that speak clearly, and that is a mistake.

Everyone tells you how excellent you are but no one is sincere by telling you how lazy and cowardly you are if you don't fight for your dream. And that's how it is; there's no need to mince words. Although that's a self-criticism, because I've been lazy and I've been a coward, at least in that aspect. I have failed over and over again by the mere fact of not trying or of giving up at the first attempt, or at the second, or at the third . . . it doesn't matter! What matters is that I didn't insist. Until I got tired of that attitude. I got tired of myself.

Luckily, I know you are not like that. You're reading this book at the moment, and you've read better ones. That's because you want to do something to change your life. You want to do something to get out of where you are and get to where you want to be. You are already getting out of your comfort zone.

But don't get used to it and rest on your laurels. There will come a time when you adapt to your new routines, your new habits, and feel comfortable again. Then you will have to find a way to keep moving forward. You can't afford to get into a new comfort zone. Always seek to be uncomfortable, because if you are not uncomfortable, you are not doing anything to move forward.

And always remember something very important:

You should be proud of what you have achieved, but never satisfied.

DO IT FOR THOSE WHO WISHED TO SEE YOU FAIL.

Here, we would also include those who, although they did not wish to see you fail, did not think you would succeed either.

Make no mistake. The main motives for success should be your desire to succeed and that it is something you like or have always wanted to achieve or obtain. You should not focus on a goal simply because others think you are not capable. This is not a matter of pride. But this is a motivational book and, once you are clear about what you want and why you want it, it never hurts to go the extra mile by showing certain people that you are capable of achieving it.

Let's be sensible, who wouldn't like to rub success in the face of that person who belittled you? I know this goes against all the theories, laws, keys, steps, and blah, blah, blah, blah, to achieve success, but it is very rewarding, at least on the inner level.

I do not pretend that you are going to prove anything to anyone or show them what you have achieved—that is not worth the effort. But you will feel better, inwardly, achieving what no one thought you would achieve. You don't need to brag about it; your success will speak for itself, don't worry about it.

> **Work hard in silence and let your success make all the noise.**

I'm just saying it's an extra motivational boost to achieve your goal. It is also quite understandable that if you have been constantly undervalued, you may consciously or unconsciously feel that you are not capable, and this type of motivation can encourage you to prove to yourself that you are capable. And I'm telling you: you are.

So remember, show those people that you are capable of anything, but do it for you. Because if you do it expecting some kind of recognition, you will be lost.

When I was in a difficult situation, I knew how bad it was because everybody made me see it. When you are like that, nobody cares about you, nobody treats you with respect—they make you feel that you are worthless. It is difficult to try to make a change, to do something productive, to change your way of being . . . because they see you and they think: "Where is this guy going? What does he think he is doing? Does he think he is going to make it? He's gone off his rocker."

And you fail, perhaps because of the simple fact that failure is inevitable, as we have seen previously. But you think you can't handle it. Sometimes not because you do not see yourself as capable, but because you believe that you are predestined to fail, that your life is not worth it, and why are you going to try? And other thoughts like that.

But there comes a time when you get tired of failing, over and over again, and of being the worst, of not being able to fall any lower, of hitting rock bottom and thinking: "Either I sink completely and forever, or I give it two shots and pull myself up like a champion." The decision is complicated, but you decide to give it courage.

It is not an overnight thing. Years go by, failures, disappointments, ups and downs, demotivation and new motivations, you fall and you get up again . . . It is like an investment graph in the stock market. If you do well, you will go up and down, winning and losing, but what counts is that the result is positive.

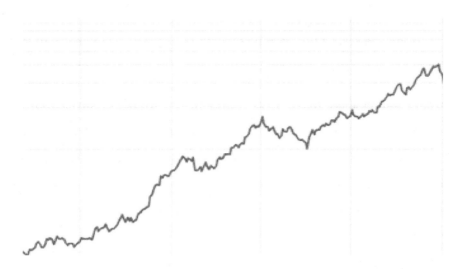

So time goes by and, despite the stumbles, you remain firm and determined to move forward. You see small progress and, as you know, "progress, even if it is slow, is still progress." And so you move forward step by step in life.

So, you go from being a failure, for whom some people give nothing, to become someone who is starting to reap some successes in life. A pretty good change, don't you think? And it just keeps going up! Once you start, you can't stop. Success wants more success.

But the point of all this: do you think anyone will give you a pat on the back? When you're at your lowest, everyone worries about making you see it, but now, do you think anyone recognizes all your effort, for all those years? Do you think anyone tells you they're proud of you? Do you think anyone is going to say "very good" to you? No one will, and let me repeat that, please:

NO ONE

Well, or maybe yes, I admit it. But you have to be prepared to deal with that kind of situation, should it arise.

I'm sure your goal is different from mine and you probably didn't start from the same point I did. If you are an entrepreneur, wanting to get to the top, you might have thought: "What the fuck is this crazy guy telling me?" But take it from me when I tell you that the scenario may be different, but otherwise, it's always the same. You'll have competitors who want to see you go down, or who don't even consider you competition because they don't value you, they don't see you as a threat. Prove that you are!

Show that you are capable of anything, but do it for you.

> **The moment they tell you that you are not good at something, it is time to prove that you are not just good, but the best.**

That the world is full of envious people and people full of bad intentions is something you won't be able to avoid. But it is up to you to rise above it all.

Ignore criticism. I once heard a line of reasoning that stuck in my mind. It was that if you want to annoy someone, ignore them. Ignoring someone who is hurting you is the most harmful thing you can do to them, and at the same time, it's the most beneficial thing for you. If you ignore them, you won't have to be bothered by what they do or say. Ignoring that person will annoy him/her more than the fact that you hate him/her and seek revenge or something similar. If you hate them, it means that you are aware of them, that they are important and that you spend time, effort, and feelings on them. Ignoring is worse for someone like that. If you ignore them, it means that they don't exist for you. They are nothing. They are nobody.

> **To those who wish me ill, I wish them long life, so they can see how far I will go.**

So, move on from those people, move on from those negative thoughts and feelings. Go on your way and do what you have to do.

Successful people do not care about the opinions of others, if it is not to take advantage of some constructive criticism. You must have a filter and select the worthless comments (which are still air) from the comments that, even if they are directed against you in an attempt to destroy you, can offer you a benefit.

Every time you receive a criticism, before getting angry, do something: stop and think for a moment, and decide if you can get something good out of that comment. Perhaps your enemy, without knowing it, is giving you the key to improve your performance.

They may tell you that you are not doing a certain thing well. You have to swallow your pride and before you say, "What do you mean I'm not doing it right?" think, "Am I really doing it right? Could I get better at this?"

If it is destructive criticism, simply, as they say, "it goes in one ear and out the other." In short: TURN AWAY FROM THAT PERSON.

> ## Since when does a wolf lose sleep over what sheep think?

If you are really 100% committed to your goal, you will have to dedicate many hours to it. You will have to sacrifice a lot of things (time with friends, movie evenings, TV series, etc.). We have already talked about that before. What I mean by that is that you are going to dedicate a lot of time, effort, and work to achieve success, and the evil tongues will be there to throw stones at you. You will see that, instead of recognizing all your sacrifice and dedication, they will tell you that you are OBSESSED.

Paradoxically, that word, at least in my experience, comes 99.99% of the time from your loved ones or, at least, the people closest to you. I will say again what I said before: I don't think they do it with bad intentions, but it is annoying.

It doesn't matter; it's more of the same. You go about your business. Don't try too hard to get others to know how you feel or how truly determined you are to succeed in your life.

I was a mess, and when I started exercising a lot, they kept telling me I was obsessed. If I went to work out, I was obsessed; if I didn't party to go early Sunday morning to work out, I was obsessed; if I didn't eat chorizo or fried food, and instead ate salad and grilled meat or fish, I was obsessed. And now that I lead an almost 100% fitness lifestyle, I seem to be more obsessed than ever. Sure, better when I was out drinking on weekends, right?

The truth is that there will also be outsiders, without any appreciation for you, who will say that you are obsessed when they see you progressing. You know: ignore those people.

If you don't find yourself in that situation, and you are lucky enough to have the full support of those around you, great! What a gain.

> **OBSESSION is the word used by the weak to define what we call DEDICATION.**

▍WRITE YOUR LIFE STORY.

Think of the rest of your life as a blank notebook. Everything that will be written in it from now on depends on you.

Do you really believe that you are predestined to something and that there is nothing you can do to avoid it? I don't. Take control of your life. It is clear that you will not be able to decide 100% of what is going to happen to you from now on. If I promised you that, it would be very frustrating every time it doesn't work out that way. But you can decide the path you want to follow and walk it to the destination of your choice.

If you are one of those who believe that destiny is written, and all that nonsense (yes, sorry, but it's nonsense), why don't you cross the street without looking? Why don't you jump out of a plane without a parachute? If it's not your moment, nothing will happen, right? Yes, I know that some people will think things like: "If I do it and die, it's because it was my destiny."

If you think so, I'm sorry to tell you that this is not your book. I'm sorry to reveal this so late in the book, but I have assumed that someone who decides to follow some recommendations to achieve success would not believe in such things. If your destiny is written, and it is to achieve success, you don't need any advice—just let time go by. If, on the contrary, your destiny is not to achieve success, do not go against the current, nor waste your time reading books to achieve such a thing.

That said, if you're a down-to-earth kind of person, let's move on.

Forget everything you've done so far. Start from scratch. Take this moment as an opportunity to change everything and decide what is going to happen in your life and what is not going to happen. Have you already decided where you want to go? From now on, all your decisions will be focused on your goal. Everything you do, think, or say will be a piece of the mechanism that will make the machine of success work.

It doesn't matter if in the past you failed, didn't try, gave up . . . All that is in the past and doesn't count. Focus on the now, and the later will come by itself.

Be the architect of your dreams. First, dream about what you want to achieve, wish for it with all your strength, and start building that dream, piece by piece, until it becomes a reality.

Decide who you want to be and write the chapters of your life story day by day.

Work hard. Have fun. Make history.
Warren Buffet

Imagine you had to write a story for a book, but there is one condition: everything you write will stay that way forever. You can't delete, correct, or modify anything.

How would you write it? Very carefully, thinking through every word, every action that happens in the story, before writing anything. You will try to make good decisions, trying not to make mistakes.

Imagine now that it is a magic book, and that everything you write in it will happen to you. Think about how you would write it, what you would add each time, what path the main character would follow, what the ending of the story would be.

Well, I'm going to tell you a secret: You don't need any magic book for that. Just get to work on your day-to-day life, on making your life story. If you act correctly, if you follow all the right steps, everything you want will happen. Magic? No, dedication.

> **The best way to predict the future is to invent it.**
>
> Alan Key

Let me ask you something. Could you tell me the names of your eight great-grandparents? I could go further and ask you the names of your great-great-grandparents, but no, I'll settle for you telling me the names of your eight great-grandparents.

What? You don't know them? Don't worry, I don't know them either. I could tell you a couple, but not all eight.

Why do you think this is happening? We are not going back that far. They are the fathers and mothers of our grandfathers and our grandmothers. I have even met one of them. My son has known three great-grandmothers and two great-grandfathers.

We don't know their names because they spent this life going from point A to point B without doing anything else but working themselves to death, and nothing else. They were born, they lived, and they died. And there they remained, one more of the many, in sad oblivion. Not even their own family knows about them. And it is a pity.

Now, do you think Albert Einstein's great-grandchildren (if he has any) don't know their great-grandfather's name? What about Abraham Lincoln's descendants?

> **If you're not going to leave a footprint,
> don't even take a step.**

Decide how you want to end up in this life, how you want your passage through it to be. Do you want to be one more, like an animal that is born, eats, defecates, grows, dies, and is never heard from again?

What are you going to do to be remembered? You don't need to reach Albert Einstein's level. And don't get confused—it's not fame you should be looking for. Maybe you are like me and you don't even want it. But do something for which you will be remembered, maybe not worldwide, but in your environment and, yes, in your family for generations.

It can be anything, as long as you do it in an extraordinary way: you can help others, invent something, start a company, be the best at whatever . . .

Do yourself a favor and do society a favor; be someone worthy of being remembered. It will be worth it. You can do it, you have the potential. Forget and eliminate any kind of mental limitation.

> **Start writing your success story today. Set your goals and follow them until they become reality. You have to believe in it even before you see it. Whatever your mind can receive and understand, it can be achieved.**
>
> Mary Kay Ash

IF YOU THINK YOU ARE PERFECT, YOU WILL NEVER BE PERFECT.

Cristiano Ronaldo

(Nike advertising spot)

Although it may seem obvious, this is a mistake that is very easy to fall into, most of the time without realizing it. I confess that I have made it myself, without being aware of it.

For years, I have researched all the topics related to my work, which is based on sports nutrition. I have gobbled up tons of information for the sheer pleasure of it. That led me, some time ago, to believe that I already knew everything, or at least almost everything in this world. I didn't hesitate to contradict certain statements, thinking I had the absolute truth in everything that was said about these subjects. And the truth is that I knew a lot. In fact, I can affirm that no one around me knew even half as much as I did. But that did not mean that I knew everything—far from it!

That was all before I started my own sports nutrition business. When I set it all up, I had some insecurities. I didn't want to find myself in a situation where a client knew more than I did, or where I didn't know how to help them at all.

So I decided to study more advanced subjects and realized that yes, I did indeed know no more than the equivalent of the tip of the iceberg. That didn't mean that I lacked extensive knowledge in my sector, nor that I was normally unlikely to provide accurate information and solutions for my type of clients, but I couldn't consider myself an expert.

I had made the mistake of thinking that I already knew it all and, therefore, I was not moving forward.

That is the problem that many of us have. We think we have mastered a certain subject and that prevents us from progressing, from achieving success, from excellence.

This is the opposite feeling of not thinking you are good enough at something. However, it is just as destructive. The one who believes that he cannot get there advances the same as the one who believes that he has already arrived.

I must tell you something, and that is that you NEVER become perfect at anything, you NEVER achieve excellence. But don't misunderstand me. Just because you can't reach it doesn't mean you shouldn't try.

You may never be perfect, but you can be much better.

You must believe that you can be the best at whatever you set your mind to, because that feeling is what produces champions.

That is somewhat contradictory but, as in everything, what you need is to know how to find a balance. Believe that you can be the best. Believe that you have everything you need to be the best. But never settle for it. You have to keep moving forward, to surpass yourself. Do you understand? Even if you're the best, you'll still have someone to surpass: yourself.

> **To improve is to change; to be perfect is to change often.**
>
> Winston Churchill

Think about the author of the phrase that gives the title to this chapter, Cristiano Ronaldo. Why is he so good at his sport? Because he is convinced that he is the best. He believes he is, but he does not rest on his laurels. He is always trying to improve, to be an improved version of himself, and to make sure that no one else takes his place.

The same goes for his "arch nemesis," Lionel Messi (I'm not going to discuss which is better of the two, because I simply don't care). He's also sure he's the best, and that's what makes him so good.

Arnold Schwarzenegger, the greatest bodybuilder of all time—not because of his seven victories as Mr. Olympia, but because of how much he contributed to the world of bodybuilding—did not doubt for a moment that he was the best of all. He would go out on stage convinced that he was going to win. In fact, he bragged about it, in a sarcastic way, to his fellow competitors. On the internet, you can see photos and videos of him wearing a T-shirt with the message, "Arnold is number one."

Throughout my life I have come across successful people with one characteristic in common. Do you know what it is? They would not allow anyone to be better than them in a certain field. Sometimes in no field at all. I really hated that attitude. I preferred to be humble and, even when I thought I could measure up to them, I preferred to be just one more. And that's what I was, one more.

Do you know what has become of these hateful people? They have important jobs, in fields they are passionate about. And they make a lot of money. Yes, I said "money." It may seem a somewhat material desire, but those who have needed it to eat, or worse, to be able to feed their children, will understand me.

It was clear to them that they had to be the best, ever since they were children.

But they didn't think they were the best, just for the sake of it. No. They had to really be the best, and not just sit on their hands along the way, avoiding being snatched away from the top.

That mentality, which some may find unhealthy (it seemed so to me) is what it takes to get to the top. Without that attitude you won't get anywhere.

I'm not talking about trampling on anyone, or anything like that. I'm just saying that you have to have the drive to get to the top. You can do it, I guarantee it. It's just a mental limitation.

Yes, I know that the chapter started talking about how you don't have to believe you are perfect and I ended up saying the opposite. And it all depends on the perspective from which you look at it.

<u>Conclusion</u>: Don't think you know everything or are the best at something, because you won't advance. But do believe that you do have the potential to approach excellence.

And remember that you will never be perfect, but you will be better. If you are already above average, aim higher. If you're already at the top, surpass yourself.

> **Aim for success, not perfection. Never give up your right to be wrong, because then you lose the ability to learn new things and move on with your life.**
>
> David D. Burns

DON'T STOP WHEN YOU'RE TIRED.
DO IT WHEN YOU'RE DONE.

A runner doesn't stop until they have crossed the finish line. No matter how tired they are, no matter how many times they stumble along the way, no matter how much they want to quit. Toxic thoughts will pop into their mind, but they know that until they have crossed the finish line, they will not stop.

On the road, or career, to success, exactly the same thing happens. Or at least it's supposed to.

If you thought it was going to be a bed of roses, you couldn't be more wrong. We have already mentioned above that, if it were, anyone would do it.

Success is reserved only for champions. Triumph awaits only those who finish the whole journey, without excuses, without regrets, without complaints, without whining.

Forget everything you have read, or heard, about the whole process being happiness, setting some goals, and getting to the top jumping for joy. Run away from promises of easy and effective guidelines to achieve your objective.

The road to success is hard, and when I say "hard," I mean really hard.

You'll have a hard time, you'll want to quit, you'll feel frustration and sometimes even social rejection. But all that only makes it more interesting,

Remember that an achiever, a successful being, does not choose the easy path, the path of mediocrity. You don't want to do the normal thing, like normal people, and be just another one of the crowd.

The successful person looks for challenges and finds possibilities where others only see impediments.

A successful person builds walls with the stones on the road, then builds momentum, jumps over those walls, and has enough strength left over to punch the wall down.

No one says it will be easy, but it will be worth it.

Never give up, ever, no matter how far away you see the goal. It's there, I promise you, even if you can't see it. You just keep moving forward and I assure you that sooner or later, you will spot it on the horizon. Then you will make one last push and cross it.

When you feel like giving up, stop for a moment and reflect. Are you at the same point you were when you started? I'm sure you're not. That's progress, dear friend.

Do you really want to throw away all your effort and sacrifice? I don't think so.

Don't let yourself be driven by the demons of failure. They will be continually trying to convince you to give up. Don't listen to them! You can feel weakness, you are human, but feeling weakness should not lead you to be weak.

Nor should you fall into the trap of taking a break. Sometimes you will feel that you are doing very well, or that you simply need a break. There are no breaks for those who want to achieve success.

> **It is forbidden to give up. Take a deep breath and keep going.**

If you start taking breaks, I can assure you, almost with certainty, that you will end up quitting. Keep in mind that this is about acquiring habits, and those habits must be productive. What kind of habits do you think you can acquire by taking a break?

I'm sorry to be so harsh in what I'm about to tell you, but that's a lazy thing to say. Are you a lazy person? Or are you a winner, with enormous, indestructible willpower? Are you not willing to give it your all? Are you not up to the task? Are you, or are you not, willing to pay the price?

I think you have all the potential. We all do. It's just a matter of getting in the right mindset. Remember that limits only exist in our mind.

Give everything for your dream. It's there, waiting for you. You just have to catch it. Bring out all the energy you have inside you, all the courage, all the desire . . . and transform yourself into a bloody, unstoppable victory-producing machine.

> **Every day, you have a new chance to keep moving forward. Every step, every triumph, every drop of sweat counts. Don't stop.**

THANK YOU

You weren't born by chance, you were born because you have a purpose,
a dream that bears your name and is inspiring you.

Bernardo Stamateas

We started the book trying to explain what success is. We even incorporated definitions of what success means to some people.

Well, for me, success, right now, lies in the thought that I may have helped you, or at least motivated you, to achieve yours.

And for you, what is success? Whatever it is, the sky is the limit.

And remember:

Shoot for the moon. Even if you miss, you'll land among the stars.

W. Clement Stone

This humble book is the result of years of failure, learning, headaches, frustration, hard work, sacrifice, and my own personal development.

I hope I have helped you and given you something of value.

Did you find it useful?

I hope you liked it and that you learned some interesting things.

I would like to ask you for a favor so that this book reaches more people—please rate it with a sincere opinion on the platform where you purchased it.

It will only take you a few seconds. With that small gesture, you will be helping me to continue with new projects.

I can't wait to start writing my next book for you!

See you soon!

www.amazon.com/dp/8409420406

Do you feel like your life is a never-ending cycle of

negative thoughts and emotions?

Do you struggle with loving yourself unconditionally?

Do you want to finally see the brighter side

of things and live a happy life?

You're not alone.

A lot of people struggle with these things. It's easy to get bogged down by negative thoughts, and before you know it, your whole day is ruined.

It's totally normal to have negative thoughts from time to time, but if they're preventing you from living a fulfilling life then it's definitely time to do something about it.

Get on the path to happiness and self-love with this book that will show you how!

You can change your mind about your problems and start to be happy with your life. All it takes is some positive thinking and a little practice.

In this book, you will:

- **Uncover the secrets to healing your inner child**
- **Silence negative thoughts and lock them away**
- **Understand the secrets to find happiness!**
- **Solve any problem you face with ease**
- **Discover your true purpose in life**
- **Bring light into your life and stay away from the darkness**
- *And more!*

With effective strategies to heal your inner child, shift your perspective, and create your own safe space. You'll never have to be victim to your own mind ever again.

Finding happiness doesn't have to be so hard anymore.

Made in the USA
Middletown, DE
07 June 2023

32198234R00056